Double Stroller Dreams

poems by

Jesse Curran

Finishing Line Press
Georgetown, Kentucky

Double Stroller Dreams

for
Leona & Valentine

and

the Schwinn Turismo
for carrying us all...

Copyright © 2021 by Jesse Curran
ISBN 978-1-64662-492-8 First Edition
All rights reserved under International and Pan-American Copyright Conventions. No part of this book may be reproduced in any manner whatsoever without written permission from the publisher, except in the case of brief quotations embodied in critical articles and reviews.

ACKNOWLEDGMENTS

"Ratatouille" in *Farmer-ish*. Vol. 1. Issue 1. Summer 2020
"To Respond," "Forsythia," and "Color Explosion" were commissioned by the Oak Spring Garden Foundation, and published in their online exhibition "Shelter in Art." May 2020.

Publisher: Leah Huete de Maines
Editor: Christen Kincaid
Cover Art: Jesse Curran and Leona Licopoli
Author Photo: Jennifer Vacca
Cover Design: Elizabeth Maines McCleavy

Order online: www.finishinglinepress.com
also available on amazon.com

Author inquiries and mail orders:
Finishing Line Press
PO Box 1626
Georgetown, Kentucky 40324
USA

Table of Contents

(Beginnings)

Double Stroller Dreams 1
Baby's First Christmas 3
On Not Watching the Eclipse 7
Levanto 9
Ode to the Great Camp 13
More 16
Cereal & Milkies 17

(Quarantine Acts)

To Respond 18
The Trump Trap 20
Forsythia 21
Water the Babies 23
Color Explosion 25
On Day 68 26

(Ends)

Mid-March 27
Leaving Ward Avenue 29
Ratatouille 30
By Way of the Way 32
The Montauk Daisy 34
Double Stroller Dreams II 35

Double Stroller Dreams

Walk with the sunscreen, snacks, and sippy cups
Walk when they tantrum, walk when they snooze
Walk when it's raining, walk when it starts to snow
Walk through humid July afternoons, gnats swarming
       in the shade of the damp oaks
Walk, stop, pick up their Ziploc bags off the pavement
Walk and scold yourself for the Ziploc bags
Walk to think and think and think and think
       and think
Walk to think there are some poets who must be parents
Walk and feel you're doing a terrible job
Walk because you're an introvert inclined to isolation
Walk because you thought you were a patient person
Walk to see the water, the boats bobbing in the bay
Walk to smell low tide, to see the sunset
Walk to watch the whitecaps peaking with the wind
Walk to check out the excavator digging in the parking lot
Walk to tell her to speak up, her sweet pixie voice
       drowned by the diesel trucks

Walk four, three, two, one mile

Walk so they sleep
Walk so you sweat

Walk because one child is like having a friend
Walk because with two children, no needs are met
Walk because the days are long, the years are short
Walk because of the clichés you've become
Walk because you sleep in your daughter's bed
Walk because she snores in the king with your husband
Walk because you sleep alone, which seems to suit you, alone
       in the purple room with the princess pillowcases
Walk because walking is the only motion
Walk for the great walkers who did their work while walking

Walk for Thoreau and Wordsworth and Woolf
Walk for Whitman walking these same jagged shores day in and day out
      year after year
Walk for those who know the body moving is divine inside and out
Walk because if you can have faith in anything, it's this
      the body the breath the sweat the sweet rhythm the pulse
Walk because there's wisdom in walking and walking
      and walking when all else fails

Walk because of the words guilt and shame and fear
Walk because you knew them before this
Walk because you know them much better now

Walk because you give up writing to walk

Walk and wonder what you'll do, how you'll walk
      when they're too big, when they won't fit in the stroller
      when they won't doze and settle like they do now

Walk so they sleep
Walk so you breathe

Walk so you can stare at them when you arrive home, asleep
      in their baby state, as you sip iced lemon water on the porch
      and finally feel like yourself again

Walk because it actually hurts to love so much—a fierceness
      beyond grasping—
Walk because they are already slipping out of this stroller
Walk because soon enough you'll once again walk
      alone

Baby's First Christmas

warm croissant
strawberry jam
lemon water, winter light

the window open
all the birds gone south
sixty-five on Long Island

green peaks of garlic
too tall, too soon
we do our best

daddy makes nonna's meatballs
I write a letter
you sleep

your new being
has me look twice
at nativity scenes

Jesus was a baby
and the wise ones
brought gifts

you know nothing of things
commerce, exchange
expectation

you know texture
color, light
the glittering tree

I hum *Silent Night*
you delight
in the crinkle of paper

you are how we should be
a Buddha, content
our best nature

buried beneath
the suffering
of wanting

of worry
of money
of things

and so
your present
is a basket

sweet potatoes and butternut squash
cosmic purple carrots
a fat fairy-tale pumpkin

they arrive on the stoop
your first foods
from friends

to be boiled
to be soaked
in breast milk

to be mashed
to be spooned
to you

grown here
they are hope
health comes

through labor, through sweat
through the fecundity
of this, our earth

everything
with a new baby
is essential

essentia
in Latin
being itself

darling
gone
are those first months

I echo
the refrain
it goes ... so quickly

I touch your hands
there is no softer softness
though never again will they be

so soft
soon you'll crawl and climb
and one day

may they callus
from some hard
real work

darling, you come to chaos
guns in schools, melting ice caps
even smarter smart phones

darling, you come
to us
full of contradiction

we watch the light
we plant berries
we work on our breath

this breath
the lemon water
the meatballs

the letters
the glistening
strawberry sweetness

yes, the manger story
there is a star
some sheep

there is
a woman
in blue

and a baby
being itself
how beauteous

you are
our beloved
our blessing

our gift

On Not Watching the Eclipse

For one day, the news is not about bigots, bombings
and battering the planet with big money.
For this day, the buzz of this spectacle, this need
to behold. Down the hill, I watch my neighbor
with his pinhole camera, his boisterous
good will. He's showing it to his loves,
Maggie and Maria. They're watching for me,
uphill, with no glasses or shoebox, only a pen
and notebook, present and unprepared.
Not seeing asks for a certain faith.
Certain and faith in the same sentence
ask for something more, a deep breath
into the moment, this moment, the tomatoes
rotting and the yellow begonia, its blossoms
far better for having been ignored.
My babies are asleep in their beds.
I can't see it, but the summer is slipping away.
We humans are so desperate for wonder
for signs, for an omen to wipe us clean.
We want something to give way—a flash
a promise or premonition that our children
will have clean water, that our careers will lift us
that our jobs won't crush us, that our places
won't plague us with loneliness
and the unstoppable sickness
of wanting more.
Soon my son will wake.
I'll let his long lips find my breast and he'll have
what he needs. I'll close my eyes and breathe
and find what I need. There is no other work.
There is a terror in seeing
and also one in not seeing.
Meanwhile, my babies are sleeping.
Maggie and Maria witness it for me
and there is this hush, this certain faith, still

in the nature we destroy, a certain faith
in the stillness
of what is happening.

Levanto

The sun goes down
on July's last Sunday

after a day of swimming
and ice cold *birra*

because it's just so hot
it's the *festa di san giacomo*

and when the sun goes down
someone, perhaps a child

places a candle in the bay
then someone drops another

then another   another
            another

a child puts in one
a man places two

his sister offers three
while slowly

his wife
adds a hundred

un'altra un'altra
        un'altra

the whole village
lights candles

they light them
for their *nonnas* long gone

they light them
for lovers that might be

they light them
for the puppy who fled

they light them for babies
lost in those first months

they light them to keep
their tattooed teenagers safe

they light
a hundred thousand

they celebrate
the patron saint of sailors

it's the *festa del mare*
the thick of summer

the spray of wax flower
bougainvillea, ice-cold *birra*

fatigue from a day swimming
disperses me

from this cliff, twenty-five meters
above the sea

and so, with some wine
some *pecorino*, some *pesto*

we watch them
bobbing on the bay

those thousands
of wishes

a whole Levanto
of longing

they flood the nocturne
with nodding light

then fireworks
sever the silence

the barking dogs
wake the baby

our baby
the one for whom, years ago

we came here
and wished to be

and after years
chasing edges

you turn away
from the extravagance

the palette of color
the power of sound

you move toward
the silent candles

they drift out to the sea
they drift into the dawn

they stay with us
they bob inside us

they become the image
my longing

longs
to be

Ode to the Great Camp
(for William D)

There is a photograph of you at Uncas.
Nineteen thirty-one, poor, aged
at a loss, lacking a place of your own.
Yet completely at ease. Your legs
casually crossed, your arm draped
over the back of the bench.
A prodigal returned, the master
a visitor, back to bask for a moment
in the world he created. *Bask*—
from the Old Norse root—to *bathe*.
So you bathe in it:
how the manor house is planted
on the high point of the peninsula.
How the windows all have sixteen panes.
How you found something in America
knowing we'll never have Chartres
or Santa Maria Maggiore
with their stained glass and softened stones
their centuries of pattering feet
and Sunday worship.
Instead, these woods—and how a home
might be made from them;
their strength and style, beams and hoists
stone chimneys and raised hearths
the split-log mantel—the outside
brought in—all the native parts
that make this place whole.

There was you, there is me.
There are almost ninety years.
There is the white pine, her twisted
trident trunk watching us both.
Her patient body still breathing
on the edge of Mohegan's depth.

When you dreamt this place
when you built the rail, then the road
when you heaved the stone
and lumbered the pines—
could you imagine us here?
Could you see the canoe drifting by?
Could you smell the chicken on the grill
or taste these icy cold cocktails?
Could you feel the forgotten pleasure
of the badminton birdie bounding into the sky?
Surely you sensed these deep sleeps
snuggled under wool blankets
the cool August nights—and maybe
you could envision the children—
my children—rolling on the pine needles
splashing in the lake, staring into the stars.
Please know that in this century
of climate catastrophe, this place
sustains them like carrots and cucumbers.
It strengthens them and teaches them
to bound, to wander, to watch
to be part of something
to be intact.

Camp from *campo*—the open space
for sport. Not that it's very open here.
The pines cloak us, but the camp
opens us. We play. We are
at ease.

If you could come back to us, come join us
for saunter around the peninsula
and tortillas on the back porch
we could find reason for belly laughter.
We would pull down a book of poems
from the shelf, read *Kubla Khan* by the fire.
Or better yet, read Whitman.
I would thank you for your vision.
How you brought greatness
to this camp. I would let you know
how this place fills us, quiets us, stills
something inside us. Maybe you couldn't
see us here, but saw the idea of us. . .
and for this, a sense of gratitude.
To be here, if only for a bit.
To sit on the bench and bask
in the seamlessness of it all.
How a home, this home
might be, profoundly
in its place.

More

Instead of me
there's them
two years, two months

two years will read you her books
but insists on reading them
all of the time

two months wants to be held
and held and held and held
all of the time

I want to give them
more of me
than there is of me

I stare at the clock
I damn the farmer husband
for when the rains come
for when the tractor breaks
for when the cucumbers rot
for what is and what is beyond
all control

outside the mint flowers
flood over the concrete steps
and as we plod by the bees
brush our ankles

these sweet-smelling
sticky babies
want more of me
than there is of me

July exhales into August
it smells like rain and more rain

I go back inside
I give them more of me

Cereal and Milkies

For well over a year, in the Winnie the Pooh bowl
each morning he takes, a scoop of Cheerios
a scoop of bran flakes, and then come the raisins
and after, the milk, to moisten and mush.

He dons the bib with the balls, lifts the blue-handled
baby spoon and feasts at the counter, swirls
on the stool like an old man in the corner café
stirs sugar into his morning cappuccino.

He smiles as he slurps, welcomes the day, such pleasure
he takes, watching the squirrels scamper, he turns
to me, points his finger—*look mommy, a red-jay*—
and I, trapped in my I, wait for my coffee

to dip biscotti, as I've done for twenty years
in the same well-loved lapis blue mug.

To Respond

Today you took out the tiller
did six passes, cutting into our front lawn
a fifteen-by-fifteen-foot square into our front lawn.
Our toddler follows with his Little Tykes
mower, mimicking each pass and turn.
After, you scatter a brown bag of seeds,
the miracle of nitrogen-fixing,
of cover crop, field peas and oats
ready to sow themselves into spring.

Neighbors pause to watch from their safe distance.
I survey from the porch, holding my own distance.

I mourned all morning and when I went to jog
my miles, it wasn't the muscles but that marvelous
Japanese word *kokoro*—the mind-heart—that felt tired.
Tilling over the morning's news of a friend
who took his own life in Liguria. The joy
of his expat existence spiraled into something
we'll never fully see. This same morning
we decide to cancel our trip to Italy,
no days this summer in Tivoli to show our son
his beloved waterfalls and fountains flowing
from the Sabine hills. So many griefs
pebbles and boulders, all with their weight.

You respond by turning earth into food.
I respond by turning tears into words.

Respond, linked to the Latin root:
to sponsor, to pledge. To make
an answer, a ritual act.

You know, when you till up the grass like that
myriad little flies swarm above the earth.

All that movement below surfaces and scatters
in the late afternoon light.

The buzzing dust of the earth cut open
before the soil settles, readying itself for new roots.

My husband, I pledge my words
to your earth.

The Trump Trap

My dear daughter
spends the afternoon
digging in the dirt.

She fills the hole with rocks.
Spends an hour heaving them
across the yard.

Then come sticks, smaller stones
layered and latticed over the top.

Finally she tears out overgrown grass
sweet onions and dandelions.

She smooths them on top,
transplants some purple
dead-nettle in the center.

Then she asks me
for a cookie, a mindful
bit of bait.

I try so damned hard
to practice compassion, to teach my kids
the just path through the dark.

But if a child
needs a bad guy
for her booby trap,

let it be one
who refuses
to grieve.

Forsythia

Legend says they can make milk.
Their yellow is so damn creamy
it almost seems possible.
I want to walk right into one.
To melt into something softer
something downier than this
damned dampness, this insistent
pandemic panic.

They used to seem to me
a can of dropped paint
color and only color.

Now, it's their buttery-ness
that beckons, draws me closer
a promise to be consumed
a saturation to silence
the rattled heaving heart.

**

In Chinese medicine, it is said
that the fruit can be used
to soften the swelling
of the lungs' small passages.
Such fruit might alleviate
the stiffness of the alveoli.

**

Every other afternoon
I lace up my sneakers
and burst out of quarantine
some small assurance in response
to this warning from beyond.

I chug up the hills, pace a few miles
breathing into knowing
this sickness
sickens the lungs.

While the heart sings of joy
the lungs are decidedly
the seat of grief.

**

It's the last day of March
a cool damp daffodil morning.
Gray and green Irish drizzle.
Memories of some place
not this one. To be situated
upon center. *Epi-kentron.*

The arteries and veins that flow
from Gotham's keens
and Gotham's woe.

**

I trot from yellow to yellow
to saffron to canary
to citron

Step by step, day by day
breath by breath

forsythia
by yolky
medicinal
forsythia.

Water the Babies

It's so bucolic I take a photograph.
The kids, two and four, soon-to-be three and five.
Him with his peach, her with her plum.
They help drag out roots and heave rocks.
They peer into the hole they just helped dad dig.
They wear oshkoshes and galoshes.
They have cherub curls and blueberry stained cheeks.
Who needs preschool when we have this?
It's actually Arbor Day and we are actually
planting trees. Twelve of them.
We are making sure they're straight,
throwing compost and manure into the hole.
Using plastic snow shovels to push the soil back
then patting it down with our chilly palms.
There are bright blue skies and marshmallow clouds.
The forsythia is bursting, and my god
how much happier the plum seems
now that she's out of her bucket.

It's so tragic I won't take a photograph.
Of how the shovel becomes a weapon.
Of how they bicker over who gets the blue one.
The little guy tantrums and whines
desperate to watch another movie.
They haven't been kissed by their grandparents.
Their bosom buddies are barricaded
down the block, while their parents
squander too many hours peering into screens
reading scientific studies of uncertainty.

Along the red fence, a peach a plum
a peach a plum a peach a cherry
a peach. And in the back, honey crisp
fuji, gravenstein, and the grand pollinator
granny smith (my beloved fruit — tart
crisp, old-soulish). Still to come,
ever-green Anjou, and that lush
thin-skinned Bartlett.

By Mother's Day, there are fuzzy donut peaches
the size of a quarters and heaps of hard green cherries
the size and look of coffee berries.
So long as we ward off the peach leaf curl
we will have fruit for our August ice cream.

Whatever happens, we do this:
we wake, eat breakfast, get dressed
brush our teeth.

We go outside.

We water the babies.

Color Explosion

She colors like the banjo player
claw hammers his way
through old time bluegrass.
She's a mad fiddler sawing the bow
through a ballad intended
to help us dance.
Her four-year-old fingers
almost crush the crayon
to achieve what she calls
color explosion.
Sometimes she double-fists.
She does this for hours.
She covers every square centimeter
of printer paper in kaleidoscopic color.
She's a scribbling woman,
sometimes sloppy
but assuredly surrendered
to the quick surging stream
of crayon heat.

When this quarantine is over, we'll be left
with a thousand pages, rainbow houses and stalky flowers
streaming hair, eyelashes, unicorns, and pots of gold.
The things she creates and the hours she gives them.
The quick music she makes pacifies me.
Her playing speaks to something instinctive
inside me.

Bless her for finding the flow.
For finding her path
for coloring a way
though this gray spring
when we stay home.

On Day 68

Was it the cardboard tube from inside the new porch rug
        you ordered with guilt from Walmart?
Was it the husband who thought to cut the tube in three, who thought
        to let the kids joust, who thought to let himself joust?
Or was it the rhododendrons dripping their sticky pink excess,
        or buxom cabbages flowering maternal solace?
Was it the poems you were reading that day: Stern's Bolero,
        Gilbert's brief, Emily's maddest joy, WCW's
        "Danse Russe"?
Or was it the room of your own where you have been fleeing
        to read such poems?
Perhaps it was the fury bubbling up in your small children,
        which you know not how to speak of—
        but for which you feel responsible?
Was it the laughter that hurt your belly?
The belly that you've been doing your best to breathe into,
        deep inhale by long exhale?
Or maybe it was the old-fashioned wisdom of the piñata
        and the punching bag?
Was it the rapture on the other side of rage?

What was it that nudged that balmy May evening
        someplace new, someplace needed?

On day 68 of quarantine
we took to sword fighting
and for an evening
our bodies broke into song.

Mid-March

Still winter, a gaping yawn
sleep deprived season
of cutting teeth, of flu hysteria.
For the moment, Val naps
and so, we paint—my dear
how I want to frame them all.
I want more wall space
to hang them. These cardstock
masterpieces you create
even as your little body fights
yet another unnamable virus.
March is full of nor'easters.
The winter drags on, relentless
runny noses, dry skin, scratchy throats.
My root-canaled tooth, they tell me
needs to be yanked.
The sticky red Tylenol, spat
back up glazes Val's hair.
How hunkered we are
in our empire of Kleenex, trapped
in our maze of garment madness—
the too snug snow boots
and all the lost mittens
and yet, as things spiral apart
there's this—Mozart—
the Piano Concerto.
Number 21 in C
thawing it into something
quite bearable.
In gray water we dip our brushes.
We watch wet snow
clump on limp earth.
The watercolors are forgiving.
Shades of blue and green, yellow
lemon hues of an Italian Summer
the bright pink bougainvillea.

At your request, I paint two purple snails
mama and baby. The baby leads
just as you lead me, far freer
in your strokes, not attached
to ideas or things, not yet mimetic
save for rainbows. For a toddler
everything's a rainbow. This
is genius. Your genius.
I'm not sentimental
with the clothes, the shoes
the pre-school cut-outs, but these—
I want them on our too crowded walls
matted, framed, hung, and praised—
each one of them.
Each one is an opus.
Your use of color and line.
I see Matisse in his chapel.
In Vence the dancers leap
the sea sparkles. This is it.
The periwinkle hyacinth
imbues our morning
paints the tissues with promise
the andante mends what is
broken inside me.
You smear the bright blue
swirl the boggy black.
The snow spins, blanketing
the globs of violet crocus
the piano springs forth.
This my dear is how we did it
how we do it, how amidst it
we make it through March,
through winter's hard end.

Leaving Ward Avenue

I have become the dreaded suburbanite
       who hollers at her kids and sometimes
       tosses plastic toys in the trash.

You see me as the angel
       who offers ruby slippers and a Cinderella gown;
       your brother sees me as the desired object
       of his most desperate separation angst.

You both were born here, in this creaking cape
       moss growing on the roof and low tide
       lurking down the hill.

In two weeks we will leave; our new old house
       is almost ready.

It is never a good time to pack, to throw away
       old photographs, dissertation notes
       blemished baby blankets.

They say moving can be like prison.
They say meaning is not in these boxes.
They say it is memory
                that keeps us warm.

Ratatouille

Slice the squash
dice the onion
tend the September bounty
tend tomatoes on the verge of rot
tend tomatoes with soft spots oozing
tend tomatoes with fruit flies teeming
enter suburban survival mode
cut the tomatoes, half-inch dice
dice because there has been no eros
dice because there have been idiopathic hives
slice because there is ceaseless chattering
about the powers of Mary Poppins
slice because there are wacky triglycerides
nebulized coughs, respiratory viruses
bounding through our babies
no matter what happens, keep dicing
dice despite sick parents
dice despite their infectious disease doctors
dice despite the hurricanes of tears
remember that despite all, you can dice
you can peel the onions
you can dice and you can slice
yellow squash, striped zucchini clubs
spoon out the seeds, chop the rest
chop because the four year old
will not potty train
chop because the two year old
can't stop pinching nipples
chop because for the rest of the week
there's cold oatmeal in the car for breakfast
chocolate-chip granola bars at your desk
for lunch—but come the weekend
a pile of sharp-stemmed eggplant
bunches of basil
sprigs of wild thyme
so you dice—

come Saturday, you peel and trim
you cleave and cube
you stack the staples
in the cast iron Cuisinart
you stir and season and sauté
you simmer a summer
on the verge of rot
you drink table wine
in splatter enamelware
the kids swing in the backyard
and friends come to toast
friends come to eat
your afternoon of dicing
the dried oak crackles in the fire pit
the crisped brown bread
soaks up the stock
this peasant dish fills our bellies
is a small salvation
an effort, a working with
the abundance
we have
and the abundance
we've been given.

By Way of the Way

We translate them as roads, but really, *via*
means way. And the way, as the Daoists say,
is the path. For me, all roads lead to Rome
or at least to Fiumicino then into a Fiat
and on to Siena and a café table
in the fanned shaped Campo.
The Romans called the Via Appia
the *Regina Viarum*—the Queen of the Roads
the road from Rome to the seas of Greece,
the bridge from one ancient world to another.
My *Regina Viarum* is more of a pilgrimage path.
A scallop shell around my neck, well-worn
hiking boots, a smartly maintained blister
and the haze of passing through landscape
as one is meant to: olive grove by olive grove,
step by step, scent of wood-smoke
and wild thyme, welcoming *un bicchiere
di vino rosso* at the long day's end.
Though these days, my *Regina Viarum*
is more aptly called the Via Domestica,
the way of dishes and laundry, lost puzzle pieces
and reshelving board books, which runs parallel
to the Via Suburbia, the way of endless emails
grocery orders, breaking up kid fights
and fetching snacks. On this path, one
marches along to the buzz of mosquitos
and the wail of the bee-stung, while inhaling
the redolence of delivery truck and pesticide
dew. Yes, my way has been the Via Typica:
college, grad school, love and loss, wobbly
academic career, two kids, mortgage,
insanity, and so forth.

On a good day I'll tell you that the journal is the way
the breath, the morning jog. Chopping the garden bounty
surrendering to the season's heat. On a good day
I'll confess that crying is the way, that kindness is all.
On a good day, I'll even concede that dishes
are the path, the cool water and the simple
confirmation of a dirty glass now clean.

And on a day like today, when the kids
watch too much crap and the San Marzanos rot
before we can make sauce, we seem
to find the way by way of the way.

Listen, there's this beach called Sand City.
It stretches a mile and has no swim lines.
In the late afternoon in late August
when the tide is high and the sun descends
it could trick you into thinking you're back
floating in some Ionian cove, having arrived
just earlier that morning on Ithaka.

Here children relinquish their puddle jumpers.
Here parents can't answer emails.
Here the banished queen comes home.

The Montauk Daisy

It's the perennial of the end in these parts
summer's last extravagance, like something
spring might grant us though riddled
with signs of autumn. Spikey leaves
and hardened stems, forest green
succulence set to endure
October's wicked ways
of rust and decay.

They're all over this town, in flowerbeds
never tended, in perennial patches planted
long ago. And in their abundance, I suspect
they're giving my husband his hives
and late night wheezing.
There are so many who worship autumn.
Shelley's west wind, Frost's nothing gold.
Keats's swallows twittering.
My college students seem settled, content
with their hoodies and hacking coughs,
but for me, with my Scorpio blood
born weeks past the equinox
it's all death and darkness.

Nipponanthemum nipponicum.
The genius of that genus, naturalized here
on Long Island, native to Japan.

Bless them for they can bear the first frost
the salty Atlantic air, the Montauk winds.
Bless them for being
at the end.

Double Stroller Dreams II

The stroller is in tatters.
The nylon is fraying between the seats
easily allowing one preschooler
to poke the other.
Not to mention the weight. Sixty pounds
split between two bellies and so many bones
makes this all a bit burdensome.

Our double stroller days are winding down.
The sun of this season is descending
into sneakers and swing sets
and skipping naps, squealing
red light, green light
as we run down the block.

Last winter, I kept seeing something terrible
striking me when I left for work—
a sideswiping truck, stress leading to stroke
inevitable tragedy born from driving
into the Long Island crucible
of cancer and car accidents.
I saw the loss life will grant them.
I saw my own fragility.

Today, the Halloween winds have stripped the dogwoods
and those creamsicle maple leaves carpet the cracked sidewalks
where we take our stroller stroll.

I knew there would be a day when this would happen.
Perhaps today is the day. The last saunter with the Schwinn.
The final tour with the Turismo.

I pray their dreams will be about mermaids and shiny fish
        singing in the seaweed.
I pray I'll be here to unstick the lolli from their silenced cheeks.
I pray that someone will always tuck the wool blanket around them.
I pray we'll all, in our ways, keep walking.

Jesse Curran is a poet, essayist, scholar, and educator who lives in Northport, NY. Her creative work has appeared in a number of literary journals including *Ruminate, About Place, Spillway, Leaping Clear, Green Humanities, Blueline,* and *Still Point Arts Quarterly.* She was the recipient of COVID-19 Artist Relief Grant from the Oak Spring Garden Foundation (2020), the Robert Frost Haiku Prize through the Studios of Key West (2013), a Pushcart Prize Nomination (2017), and an award from the Dorothy Sargent Rosenberg Poetry Prize (2013). Her scholarly criticism theorizes the regenerative relationships between contemplative pedagogy, ecological thought, and American poetry. She teaches in the First Year Experience program at SUNY College at Old Westbury. Jesse is also a certified hatha yoga instructor and permaculture designer, two practices which inform her approach to education, sustainability, and community building. She is the mother of two bright stars, Leona and Valentine. For more about Jesse's work, visit her website: www.jesseleecurran.com

www.ingramcontent.com/pod-product-compliance
Lightning Source LLC
LaVergne TN
LVHW041553070426
835507LV00011B/1065